© Okosun, Kazeem Oai

All rights reserved. E excerpts, this book reproduced in part or in whole in any manner whatsoever without the written permission of the publisher.

Unless otherwise stated all scriptures, quotations are taken from the King James Version.

Alphamight LLC
kazeemo@100bconline.com

Disclaimer

The author based the writings in this book on his entire Bible understanding. It is not written for or against any nation's or country's constitutional belief; nor is it written to condemn any individual or group of peoples beliefs.

This book is mainly for individuals who believe the totality of the Bible, want to know more about the principles of the Kingdom of God and want to gain a deeper understanding of the Bible.

So, read on if what you want to hear is the biblical truth whether it hurts or not.

Disclaimer	**1**
Preface	3
Chapter 1	6
The Inherent Power in a WOMAN	**6**
Chapter 2	43
Woman is Help Meet	**43**
The secret of oneness	49
Chapter 3	63
Wealth, honor, and glory transfer	**63**
King David as a case study	67
Pharaoh, Sarah, and Abram	75
Abimelech, Sarah, and Abram	77
Chapter 4	**80**
Generational Impacts of Kings' Adulterous Acts	80
Rebecca and Isaac Case study	80
Joseph a beneficiary	83

Preface

If we all agreed that Jesus Christ came to restore man back to his original position and glory before the fall of Adam and Eve. Then the question now is, before the fall of man was Eve subjected under the authority of Adam or was she at equality level with Adam. *Woman thou hath loosed forever* intend to provide insights into this question.

Jesus at no time discriminated against women. They were fully involved in his ministry. The first eye witness account of Jesus's resurrection was by a woman and so she by that experience was a qualified APOSTLE. And so, apostolic office is never ordained for men only. WOMEN are joint heirs along MEN with CHRIST. However, a woman who is in the spirit won't struggle with headship of the home even though she shares equality with man. She will never consider equality with man something to take advantage of or to be grasped irrespective of what the laws of the land says.

A woman should let the same mind be in her that was in Jesus Christ and then be humble in total submission to her husband as unto the Lord. Then God would exalt her above her peers and give her a name among the mighty and great men.

<u>Philippians 2: 5 - 7</u>

Let this mind be in you, which was also in Christ Jesus: Who, being in the form of God, thought it not robbery to be equal with God: But made himself of no reputation, and took upon him the form of a servant, and was made in the likeness of men: And being found in fashion as a man, he humbled himself, and became obedient unto death, even the death of the cross. Wherefore God also hath highly exalted him, and given him a name which is above every name:

Love, respect, honor, and obedience will not be an issue if the Holy Spirit is involved. Therefore, any woman with the same mind like Jesus, can be used of God and empowered to operate in any spiritual office.

Chapter 1

The Inherent Power in a WOMAN

The bible is the ACTS of God. God created man from the dust of the earth. He then took a rib from the man to form the woman. This is not all, with all similarities between man and woman, God added extras to the woman, such as the WOMB inside them, their head has ability to grow longer hairs than man, and their breasts fashioned with milk. Now let us look at the significance of these abilities in a woman scripturally.

- In the bible, grown or growing hair symbolizes the level of power or strength or anointing or grace that God placed on an individual. This is why the Nazarene were not permitted to shave their hair, because the longer it grows, the more powerful they are. For example, Samson and other Nazarene.

<u>Ezekiel 16: 7</u>

I have caused thee to multiply as the bud of the field, and thou hast increased and waxen great, and thou art come to excellent ornaments: thy breasts are fashioned, and thine hair is grown, whereas thou wast naked and bare.

- Breasts fashioned with milk, which signified spring of life or sign of life. Ability to sustain life and a fertile land. When God curses a woman with barrenness, He gives them dry breasts. God likened a barren land to dry breasts and a womb that miscarried.

<u>Hosea 9: 14</u>

Give them, O LORD: what wilt thou give? give them a miscarrying womb and dry breasts.

- The WOMB is like a mini earth (land) implanted inside a woman. Just as the earth can multiply and cloth any seed planted in it with fresh flesh or skin, stem (bone), and as the earth has the strength to sustain life. The woman' womb specifically could bring forth both male and female which has life to produce after his kind. See for instance, the ability of the earth (land) as demonstrated in the book of Genesis.

<u>Genesis 1: 11</u>

And God said, Let the earth bring forth grass, the herb yielding seed, and the fruit tree yielding fruit after his kind, whose seed is in itself, upon the earth: and it was so.

God ordained the woman to help meet Adam' needs. Eve was to help him increase, multiply his seeds, and help fulfill Adam's desires and needs. She was to be to Adam what the earth (land) is to God. That is, the earth responding positively, by bringing forth all God desired to see. We can say that Earth is "help meet" because all that God desired, created, and wanted came forth to existence from the womb of the Earth.

Therefore, with the earth and its abilities and strengths generated in the womb of the earth to produce, multiply and clothes seeds, the longer hair attributes, and the breasts show that the woman in a sense was made of stronger abilities and influence than man but excluding the strong bones, power, or might in man. Life is not by strong bones, for the race is not to the strong and not by power and not by might but by the Spirit.

Just as a man plants seeds in the ground (earth), for the earth to help increase and ensure sustenance, the man is expected to give or plant what he desires to see increased or multiplied as a seed in the woman to help reproduce. To make the land produce or fertile, you must **trust it**, cultivate, remove torn, water and nourish it. So also, we need to treat women the same way. Give her free hands to break forth, even as she submits to her lord (husband).

Therefore, when Adam said, she was the flesh of my flesh and bones of my bones, he probably saw correctly and understood that the woman was made of greater abilities than him.

Due to the sins committed by the woman, which resulted in her being subjected under the lordship and authority of man. She was bowed down and could no longer stand straight before a man and she was deprived of the spiritual capacity to stand shoulder-to-shoulder with man. We would look into this in more detail later.

The curse on a man was that he would sweat to eat from the earth, not the woman, she cannot sweat to eat from the fruits of the earth. For the earth and woman shared similar grace, mutual connections, and relationship. Because the WOMB in a woman is a mini earth planted in her by God. Women can get whatever they desire with little or no effort or no pain, the earth will bring it forth or cause the man to labor for it and the woman will just draw from the man without a hitch. Woman and earth have a lot in common and exhibit the same attributes as seen in Proverbs 30.

Proverbs 30: 15 - 16

The horseleach hath two daughters, crying, Give, give. There are three things that are never satisfied, yea, four things say not, It is enough: The grave; and the barren womb; the earth that is not filled with water; and the fire that saith not, It is enough.

Friend, this is why the earth will always help the woman, when she is in need. Just as in the book of Revelation

Revelation 12: 16

And the earth helped the woman, and the earth opened her mouth, and swallowed up the flood which the dragon cast out of his mouth.

You see, in Genesis 1, God created heaven and the earth, the earth was a virgin ground, it had never produced before that time and neither was a seed planted in it but God called forth all things created from the womb of the earth as the Holy Spirit hover or overshadowed it. That is a pointer to what God did in virgin Mary and caused her womb to birth Jesus Christ when the Holy Spirit overshadowed her without any prior seed of a man implanted in her.

One other interesting thing about the earth and her abilities is whatever you plant in it multiplies and since the dead are usually buried inside the earth (land), what the earth multiplies back from death are in the form of diseases, afflictions, infirmities, and more death. Note, when you also afflict your woman, she multiplies back to you more afflictions. Because that is what you planted.

This might likely be the reason why Jesus who is life cannot stay in the grave forever. Otherwise, the earth would be producing both death and life at the same time. In other words, this earth would have the ability to exist forever or live forever. This is the same reason God sent man out of Eden, to avoid the situation where man can live forever after sinning. For God did not want both death and eternal living to cohabit at that time on earth.

Gen 3: 22 – 23

And the LORD God said, Behold, the man is become as one of us, to know good and evil: and now, lest he put forth his hand, and take also of the tree of life, and eat, and live forever: the LORD God sent him forth from the garden of Eden, to till the ground from whence he was taken.

Hence, Christ would never allow that to happen. For this reason, a new earth and a new heaven would descend from heaven when Christ returned.

Jesus said that the children of this world are wiser than the children of the Kingdom. The devil, sensing the role and impact of women in the last days, he removed the restrictions or barrier that is against women in the society so that he can use, confuse, pollute, and corrupt them before the church wakes up to realities.

One very interesting detail found in Proverbs 31: 10 – 31 about the attributes of a virtuous woman explains it all.

Proverbs 31: 10 – 11, 30

Who can find a virtuous woman? for her price is far above rubies. The heart of her husband doth safely trust in her, so that he shall have no need of spoil.... Favour is deceitful, and beauty is vain: but a woman that feareth the LORD, she shall be praised.

The woman performs exceedingly when the heart of her husband safely trusts her and then the man shall lack nothing, all his desires shall materialize. For he shall draw from the secret grace called "help meet" hidden in her by God. If she fears the Lord, she should be praised and celebrated.

What a virtuous and godly woman needs is TRUST. We must learn to trust our women as Christ trusts the church as his virtuous bride. Unfortunately, the church has placed so many restrictions and obstacles in the ways and activities of women in the body of Christ. Instead of allowing God fearing and submissive women to explore and subject themselves to the optimal use of God. We demonized them all, calling them Jezebel for daring to demonstrate unusual grace. Forgetting that both men and women are prone to errors and satanic influences. It is not just a woman's problem, like the Lord pointed out in the book of Revelation, where Jesus referred to doctrines of Jezebel and Balaam.

Revelation 2:14

But I have a few things against thee, because thou hast there them that hold the doctrine of Balaam, who taught Balac to cast a stumbling block before the children of Israel, to eat things sacrificed unto idols, and to commit fornication.

Revelation 2:20

Notwithstanding I have a few things against thee, because thou sufferest that woman

Jezebel, which calleth herself a prophetess, to teach and to seduce my servants to commit fornication, and to eat things sacrificed unto idols.

In the body of Christ (the Church), we only have Jesus as the only male figure (bridegroom) while in the whole body, the church is the bride. If we are then all bride, there is no male or female regarding the spiritual things. We are the same as angels, according to Luke 22: 34 – 36. No gender classifications in the kingdom of God and the body of Christ.

In the Mount of transfiguration, Moses and Elijah were seen ministering to Jesus, delivering a message from the Father to Jesus. You agree with me that this was the role angel Gabriel used to play. For Moses and Elijah were as angels in the Kingdom of God. God sent men like us from heaven who once lived on earth as angels to minister and deliver the thoughts and plans of God to Jesus.

The woman with the male child in the book of Revelation and the seed of the woman as mentioned in Genesis 3 are symbolic and spiritually discerned. It is an indication and a pointer of what God intends to do through a woman's seed, ability, strength, or grace in the last days.

The ministry of the woman is important to God in His scheme of things to dislodge the Devil, bruise his head and that of his evil forces. Has it ever occurred to you that ever since the world removed the restrictions against women in society, the world has broken forth into a high level of innovations and scientific discoveries, which has changed the dynamics and fortune of the world forever. This is not a coincidence at all.

The Devil is busy pulling the women out of the church into the world because the church won't let the women breath or manifest in the lord. Subduing and putting on them heavy yoke beyond what is necessary, and of course they end up becoming a tool in the Devil's hands for sins.

The church must trust that God is able to sustain and preserve any woman He uses extraordinarily.

Just like Moses had good intentions for giving the laws, but the Israelites used the same law to hinder the move and the authority of God. In this same manner, the church and the leaders today are using some scriptures or epistles of the apostles as a stumbling block against the move and the plans of God in these last days. The Good News is that God cannot be stopped. God will dismantle all obstacles and bypass them, while He moves in an unexpected direction that would daze everyone and the world in general.

The curse and the restoration of woman

Back to the curse that God placed on the woman in Genesis, part of the pains God inflicted on Eve (the woman) for her sins brought the woman under the rule or authority of man and she lost her right to personal desire.

Gen 3: 16

Unto the woman he said,

i. I will greatly multiply thy sorrow and thy conception.

ii. in sorrow thou shalt bring forth children; and

iii. thy desire shall be to thy husband, and

iv. he shall rule over thee.

Since that time carnal men have maintained the culture of exercising rule or authority over women. The curse or judgment God placed on Eve were pains and demotion, "thy desire shall be to thy husband, and he shall rule over thee". In the beginning it was not so, otherwise God would not have added these to her punishments.

For Eve and Adam were partners, joint heir with equal rights and access to the things or grace of God. Neither was lording over the other partner. They submitted themselves (listened) one to another (Ephesians 5:21). In partnership is equality but in marriage is equity and one must lead the team. In this case man began to lead.

Our God is awesome, He has the power and ability at any point in time to waive any curse or punishment for any one or nation. Just as He terminated the power of death over Enoch, Elijah, and gave us eternal life through Jesus. He can disable, disarm, or make of no effect the curse placed on Adam or Eve in the life of any person. God is sovereign, bigger than anything, anyone has ever experienced or written or documented in any book.

Note, that the curse was not to disarm or disempower or reduce the power of influence inherent in Eve but subjected it to Adam's approval. The curse can only be broken or lifted by God, no man and no Devil can break a curse from anyone whom God has cursed. Therefore, if a woman suddenly assumed joint rulership or leadership over or with a man, it means the curse must have been lifted or broken by God. The woman is loosen from the curse. And, God has something to do and won't let any man's restrictions hinder Him.

When we give our lives to Jesus Christ, we are counted worthy of the kingdom of God and the resurrection from the dead. Christ came to restore man (man & woman) to what we enjoyed before the fall of man in the garden of Eden. Little wonder Jesus said in Luke 20: 35

But they which shall be accounted worthy to obtain that world, and the resurrection from the dead,

i. neither marry, nor are given in marriage

ii. Neither can they die any more

For they are equal unto the angels; and are the children of God, being the children of the resurrection.

So, before God Almighty, in Christ Jesus, no man, no woman. We are likened and seen as the same as angels in His Eye. This is why Jesus in the book of Revelations, chapters 2

& 3, while addressing the leaders of the churches, imperfect leaders so to say, and imperfect congregation, including those with false or wrong teachings or doctrines, he still called them angels. This is not in any way to support false teachings but to magnify the sovereignty of Almighty God.

Revelation 2:1, 12, 18

Unto the angel of the church of Ephesus write.... And to the angel of the church in Pergamos write.... And unto the angel of the church in Thyatira write....

Revelation 3:1, 7, 14

And unto the angel of the church in Sardis write.... And to the angel of the church in Philadelphia write.... And unto the angel of the church of the Laodiceans write....

Christ elevated the believers (man or woman) to angelic status, that was what they were, for they were His, until God judged them and there is no longer a chance for them to repent.

There was a particular woman (NOT women) in Revelation 2: 20 – 23 who the Lord called Jezebel because God gave her a chance to repent, and she repented not, and she was judged, and her case finalized. She was cast into a bed, great tribulations and her children killed.

Therefore, since we attained angelic status before God, we are neither male nor female, we are not judged by our physical appearance or body. God can assign anyone into any office, in any capacity irrespective of their sex as He deem fit. For whatever, God has clean or counted worthy, who are we to call them unclean or unworthy.

Jesus prophetically loosened woman from the curse placed on her in the book of Genesis when she sinned, when she was bowed, subjected to the authority of man and counted unequal to man. In a marriage relationship, the woman in reverence to God honors her man as her head. But in such a relationship is partnership rather than marriage, the woman is not obliged to submit. But they can both reach agreement as to who leads because someone must take responsibility. In the kingdom of God and the church, both men and women are joint heirs and partners. Who leads would be by mutual understanding.

In a football team or any other sports, they work as a team and then one person is appointed a captain over the rest, so when critical decisions have to be made, after consulting with the team mate, the captain's decision is final. Same thing in airplanes, with two airplane captains, one of them is responsible for the final decision. So, my take is even though it's teamwork and efforts, one person must lead or take final decisions. If the husband and wife both agree that the wife leads or should have the final say, so be it.

Luke 13: 11 – 13

And, behold, there was a woman who had a spirit of infirmity eighteen years, and was bowed together, and could in no wise lift up herself. And when Jesus saw her, he called her to him, and said unto her, Woman, thou art loosed from thine infirmity. And he laid his hands on her: and immediately she was made straight, and glorified God.

When Jesus said, woman thou art loosed, he was not only talking to the woman with the infirmities but was also prophetically healing the woman in the book of Genesis 3:16. Jesus straightening her up, launched and restored her to the same status with man, just as they were in the garden of Eden before man sinned. As a partner and co-laborer in Eden serving and submitting willingly to one another as unto the Lord not as unto man.

If God can use a donkey to rebuke Balaam, is it a difficult thing for Him to use any woman in the apostolic office? If God can raised an army for Himself from the valley of dry bones or dead people, bypassed the unwilling living army of Israel. Is it a difficult thing for Him to raise a woman in the apostolic office. If God in His sovereignty counts any woman worthy of apostolic ministry or grace, no man on earth can unworthy her. God owns the church and it's in His sole power to set people in offices, He decides the appropriate instrument(s) whether male or female He wants to use.

For anything that is controversial, the testimony of two or three witnesses is required to establish the matter. Not one witness's testimony in two or three epistles or three locations or three times (2

Corinthians 13:1). If the matter is not established, therefore, it is an open case. God can shock you by doing new things or move in a new direction that you will never believe is God at work. The Bible is the ACTS of God, it also testifies about Jesus Christ. It is not all that is about God.

John 5:39 - 40

Search the scriptures; for in them ye think ye have eternal life: and they are they which testify of me. And ye will not come to me, that ye might have life.

The Pharisees so much idolized the written scriptures that they missed Christ himself. This is the same thing the church is doing today by searching the bible hoping to by doing so have eternal life while they missed connecting with Jesus Christ directly and his unbiased nature.

Luke 24:25 - 27

Then he said unto them, O fools, and slow of heart to believe all that the prophets have spoken: ought not Christ to have suffered these things, and to enter into his glory? And beginning at Moses and all the prophets, he expounded unto them in all the scriptures the things concerning himself. (emphasis is mine)

God is way bigger than any experience of any man or apostles. Because apostle Paul said he permitted no woman in the church to have rule or authority over man, is not or never an authoritative statement that God cannot or can never set a woman in offices, whether apostolic, prophetic, pastoral, teaching or evangelistic. Apostle Paul saw in parts; he did not see all that God had in mind regarding the church and how God intended to move or use the church in the later days. For we all see in parts. God is awesome, He keeps breaking new grounds every day, the wise must be confused. God is the same yesterday, today and forever, but His manifestations are not the same from generations to generations (not the same way yesterday, today, and forever).

Please take note that God in ancient times, at times permitted the prophets to set rules, though not directly from Him but if they saw it right to help them manage their congregations. Those rules even though they became laws in Israel, they still did not originate from God Himself. That was why the Pharisees were in error, they did not know the power of God or which of the laws was from God and which laws were from the prophets.

For instance,

i. Divorce and issuance of divorce certificate: - for hundreds of years the Pharisees thought it was God's perfect will to divorce and that the law was given by God. Until Jesus told them it was from Moses (because of their hardened hearts) not from God.

ii. Manna: - for several years the Pharisees thought it was Moses that gave them manna in the wilderness. Until Jesus told them it was from the Father not from Moses.

iii. Mountains: For thousands of years, they thought mountains cannot be moved, that is, mountains are unmovable, but Jesus came and taught them that you can say unto this mountain be thou remove and it shall be move

You can be a minister or have been teaching for years and still be wrong in some teachings or revelations. Recently, for example, Pastor Kumuyi admitted having taught some doctrines that were wrong or not inline with the will of God, so also Pastor Benny Hinn and Pastor Creflo Dollar admitted they have taught some wrong doctrines. They are correcting themselves after several years of misleading the congregations. They are still angels of their various churches or still God's servants until God judges them otherwise.

Apostle Paul set the rule in his wisdom based on the family culture at that time and to Corinthians church which had a large number of Jews, to help manage the church and the type of people he was dealing with. He was probably trying to prevent situations where culture collides with church liberty. God is not however limited; you cannot help Him. He will suspend all your rules and laws at the right time when he wants to move in a way to confound the wise. If any of our rules is standing in His way, He will trample upon them, for they are like trees not planted by my Father in heaven that must be uprooted. To think that God is bound by what a prophet says is deceitful, God is only bound by what originates from Him and also permits whatever He deems fits.

The Jews never believed what God did in the New Testament could happen, because it was totally contrary to what the Old Testament (the laws and the prophets) taught them about God. They thought they could put God in a box. This same mindset is still affecting our generation today. People want to box God by an apostles' or prophets' or pastors' experiences or imaginations.

What is amazing is that whatever wonders that were wrought in a man's apostolic ministry can also happen in a women's ministry. For God is the one working in both and no one is sufficient of himself or herself to do anything. In all Christ is preached.

Peter and Ananias: Acts 5:5

And Ananias hearing these words fell down and gave up the ghost....

Abigail and Nabal: 1 Samuel 25:37

But it came to pass in the morning, when the wine was gone out of Nabal, and his wife had told him these things, that his heart died within him, and he became like a stone. And it came to pass about ten days after, that the LORD smote Nabal, that he died.

So, what happened in Apostle Peter's ministry also happened in the ministry of Abigail. It does not matter whether you are Apostle Peter or Ms. Abigail, it was God that worketh in all. No doubt, a WOMAN can be an apostle if you know the power of God.

Has it ever occurred to you that in a home, the one that is the strongest or the lead is always the devil's target?. The Devil understands the acts of war, once the strongest is captured or weakened, the others or followers become weaklings. They will all submit to the enemy once their leader is captured. Strike the shepherd the sheep will scatter, so the saying.

This is why the devil went for Eve first, not Adam, because the Devil knew that she was the strongest and the most influential in Eden. Once Eve falls Adam is also captured.

Safety net, if a woman's curse is broken, she must in the fear of God submit or influence her husband out of love or reverence for God and not as a cursed Eve that was subjected to Adam in a cursed state. If you have such a woman, rejoice, for God has been favorable to you, prosperity is upon you but if you have an unruly or not submissive woman, pray my brother, for hell is knocking. Don't force yourself to rule her, you won't win the battle.

Marriage or being married is not a criterion or a must in the Kingdom of God. Otherwise, Jesus and Paul would have married also. What is important to God, are the people who do His will. The people who do the will of God are your brothers, sisters, husbands, wives and family. Not your natural blood lines.

Jesus said that he who must follow me, must deny his father, mother, sisters, brothers to enter the kingdom of God. Apostle Paul also said let him, that is married live as unmarried. God loves family, but it is not a criterion for the advancement of the

Kingdom of God. If God can use a virgin to birth Jesus, He can use any unmarried or married individual to advance His work.

In the kingdom of this world, men marry and are given in marriage but in God's Kingdom, no marriage, we are equal to the angels.

Jesus acknowledged the outstanding faith of two people in the bible. The centurion (man) and the woman whose daughter was possessed by the devil.

Matthew 8: 9 -10

For I am a man under authority, having soldiers under me: and I say to this man, Go, and he goeth; and to another, Come, and he cometh; and to my servant, Do this, and he doeth it. When Jesus heard it, he marvelled, and said to them that followed, Verily I say unto you, I have not found so great faith, no, not in Israel.

Matthew 15: 27 – 28

And she said, Truth, Lord: yet the dogs eat of the crumbs which fall from their masters' table. Then Jesus answered and said unto her, O woman, great is thy faith: be it unto thee even as thou wilt. And her daughter was made whole from that very hour.

In another instance Jesus called a woman the daughter of Abraham. Before this time, females were not mentioned as daughters of Abraham, nor were they ever counted or acknowledged as Abraham's daughters, as the sons were talked about. Jesus using this phrase places man and woman in the same covenant of faith and the blessings of Abraham.

Luke 13:10 - 16

....and ought not this woman being a daughter of Abraham, whom Satan hath bound ...

In the scripture, we have seen the great sensitivity of some women to rightly discern what God is doing, about to do or already do while the men were not even picking the signals from God at all. I would highlight some instances below for our enlightenment.

- Sarah: Sarah rejecting Ismael' jointly inheriting the promise and blessings of Abraham with Isaac. While Abraham did not have that insight until God told him that Sarah is right.
- Rebecca: She had discerned that the promise was for Jacob and not Esau. Isaac didn't know until his plan to bless Esau backfired.
- Jacob and his wives: Leah and Rachel gave their maids to Jacob and helped him to attain the number of tribes (that is, 12 tribes) that God ordained that Jacob bear. Jacob was not discerning that at all.

- Abigail: She was able to discern that God was going to deal with Nabal Himself and not for David to stain his hands with blood. David did not pick that revelation at all.

- Mary and Martha: They were able to draw out virtues and impactful revelation from Christ when Lazarus died. Like "I am the resurrection and the life…."

- The woman by the well in John 4: successfully pulled out a great revelation from Jesus by the questions she asked. By her we know that they that must worship the Father, must worship in spirit and in truth, for God seeks for such worshippers.

- Prophetess Deborah picked the mind and the victory before Barak sensed the move of God.

It is time that the church trusts the woman and stop assuming that the callings and the fivefold ministry are exclusive to man. When a woman perceived that she is trusted and unrestricted as to what potentials she can explore, she easily expressed her gifts to the full benefit of the church and mankind.

There are two things and yea three of which flow the issues of life. The earth, the womb and the heart. These three have the abilities to conceive and produce whatever you plant into it in multiple folds. Women possessed two of the three.

Chapter 2

Woman is Help Meet

God has the habit of hiding gold and treasures in an unusual place. Treasures' natural hidden place is the earth. So also, great treasures are hidden in the woman.

When some see a woman, what they see is sex object, or they see evil creation, they likened them to Jezebel, or the devil's tools for the downfall of a man. But the wise see a woman and see HELP MEET, they see treasures and with trust tapped into the woman and they dig out fortunes, treasures and forever no longer lack spoils.

Trust and openness (keep no secret) with joy so shall you draw strength and treasures from the woman. That is, joyfully trust and joyfully share secrets. For a woman to bring forth her best and her full strength she and her husband must joyfully trust each other and joyfully also share secrets with each other and joyfully forgive each other.

Women rule the home, not their husband while the man rules the field or the open, in the city hall, or open court. Man's joy is to be respected and treated as the king who rules. Man hates open disgrace, open challenge, and disrespect from women. For instance, we can learn from these events recorded in the Bible.

- Sarah gave her maid Hagai to Abraham, God did not intervene (if Abraham and Sarah were okay with it) as to how they run their homes. Sarah later demanded that Hagai and Ismael be sent out of their home. God did not rebuke Sarah He simply counsel Abraham to comply. Because women rule the home, and Sarah's thought aligned with the mind of God on the issue.

- In the book of Esther, a queen disrespected her king openly. No one cared how she treated the king in private but in the open, it is not acceptable! The king's ego was dismantled and so the chiefs requested the queen to be replaced to prevent situations where their wives would disrespect them in the open if the queen is spared.

The strength and the glory of the man is the field (in the open). While the strength and the glory of the woman is home. This is what is displayed in the book of Proverbs 31. The man sits with friends and elders in the city hall enjoying honor and respect accorded him by his wife. Not minding how she treated him in the secret (home).

God never instructed Adam to rule or tame Eve his wife. God's command was to Eve "your desires shall be for your husband, and he shall rule over you" in other words you shall submit to him. Little wonder the bible says "wives submit to your husbands and husbands love your wives (not husbands rule or tame your wives). When God created man in Genesis Chapter 1, He commanded them (male and female) to subdue and dominate the earth and all what He created. Not that they subdue or dominate each other.

You cannot enforce or force submission from a woman. Stop trying to tame or control or subdue or domesticate a woman or wife. For these are exactly what the church and men are doing to their women today. It is what she must willingly obey as unto the Lord who gave the command. Man is not entrusted to force himself to rule or to be submitted to by a woman. Man is not a law enforcement agent. God who gave the law enforces the law and punishes offenders.

This is like a case of traffic lights and motorists. Motorists must obey or submit to traffic lights' rules and instructions. And not that traffic lights obey motorists. If motorists break the laws, then the law enforcement agents take actions. The man is like traffic lights, while the woman is like motorists. When a motorist indicates the direction and action they want to take, the traffic lights either give a green light (go ahead) or red light (no, hold on, stop action) and amber or yellow light (yes or no situation). Note that a red light does not mean rejection but it's just not the right time now.

Your desires shall be for your husband not against him. Do not desire anything that would harm him in any way emotionally or physically. A woman experiences pain and torn from earth once she assumes a man's position or wants to be in the field and not in her domain. The field is man's domain.

As a virtuous woman is to the husband, the church should also be to Christ who sits in heaven in the council of elders.

The Pharisees idolized the teachings of Moses and the laws of the prophets to the extent that when God was speaking, they resisted Him vehemently. Yet they searched the scriptures for Christ hoping to find Him and then rejected him when he arrived in their midst.

Today's church also has idolized the bible, the teachings, and the experiences of some apostles. They have exalted them above God. And when God is speaking, or doing something new, they gang up against Him. God is bigger than the entire bible (both Old and New Testaments). He is bigger than any experience any man or people had experienced in the bible. The bible is not all that is about God so stop limiting Him. God cannot be limited by the experience of any man. The bible should be used as a guide to God and His ways, not as a substitute for God.

I see a strong generation of believers branching out of Pentecostal church such as Martin Luther pulled out of the Catholic Church.

The secret of oneness

When Adam was formed, he was in the complete image and likeness of God. But then, God took from his side a rib to Eve. At that point in time I believe that Adam was no longer a complete image because a portion of that image is Eve. That is, the completeness of Adam as the image of God is Eve. When the two of them come together, they shall become one, that is, one image of God and whatsoever they shall do, dominion is certain and overcoming the devil is sure.

When God created man, He charged them to dominate and subdue the earth. The only way that can be achieved is for man to be a full, complete image of God in order to be able to defeat the devil and overcome the devil's temptations. Because, let thy will be done on earth as it is done in heaven which implies that as God rules and dominates the heavens. Such image and likeness of God combined with His abilities must be replicated on earth if the devil must fail on earth as he failed in heaven.

Genesis 1: 26 – 27

And God said, Let us make man in our image, after our likeness: and let them have dominion over the fish of the sea, and over the fowl of the air, and over the cattle, and over all the earth, and over every creeping thing that creepeth upon the earth. So God created man in his own image, in the image of God created he him; male and female created he them.

The Devil's defeat was guaranteed if Adam and Eve were united (oneness means a complete image and likeness of God). Note that if the Devil's had tempted Adam and not Eve, Adam would still have fallen into the lies of the Devil because he was no longer a complete image. For Eve was Adam's helpmeet and together with Eve was he a complete image.

When someone looks alike, it means in his likeness but not the same image. Moses built a temple of the same image of what God showed him in heaven. Assuming a part or section of the temple Moses built was cut off or defamed, it will still have the likeness (look alike) of what he saw but not the same image of what he saw.

This was what happened to Adam when a rib was taken out of him to form Eve. Adam still had the likeness of God but he was no longer the express image of God. So, when Eve and Adam come together, they become one, that is, one express image of God. This is the secret of oneness and whatsoever they jointly do, they shall have dominion and succeed in all.

Note that God from the beginning never designed Adam to be self sufficient, Adam would be complete and self sufficient when he merged with Eve. Unfortunately, sin crept in, man and woman perpetually disagree and ununited.

Therefore, God sent Jesus (the second Adam), He kept him intact, no second Eve was formed out of him. So that Jesus remained His complete image and likeness and wrapped with the abilities of God. Hence, he was able to face temptations and also defeated the Devil.

Little wonder the bible said about Jesus that in him dwells the complete Godhead. Instead of forming a second Eve, God only multiplied Jesus in the lives of believers to subdue and dominate the earth. The Holy Spirit only planted the seed (Jesus Christ) in our hearts.

<u>Colossians 1: 15, 19</u>

Who is the image of the invisible God, the firstborn of every creature:,,, For it pleased the Father that in him should all fullness dwell;

All the fullness (complete image and likeness) of God was in him. Hallelujah!

Colossians 2: 9 - 10

For in him dwelleth all the fulness of the Godhead bodily. And ye are complete in him, which is the head of all principality and power:

A woman with treasures will divinely pull the hidden resources and wealth in her to the man she loves. If she loves her siblings more than the husband for any reason, then her siblings will be more resourceful and creative to succeed more than the husband.

Our mothers were help meets, but our fathers did not know and never saw it either. In my parents' days or times and generation, women were maltreated, afflicted, oppressed, suppressed and abused with no one daring to save or protect them.

so, many women ended up staying in marriage even though there was no love towards their husband, their natural affection and love remained or geared towards their siblings with whom they shared love from childhood. As a result , poverty was prevalent among such homes and lives of abusive husbands.

Those days, while the woman's families prospered fairly, the abusive husband wallowed in abject poverty. Abusive husbands lose their wealth in unexplainable ways and poverty is directly correlated. Poor nations or continents have the same thing in common, Study poor nations today, you will be shocked to see the level of women abuse in those countries.

Abuse can be emotional, physical, or sexual etc. Little wonder the poverty rates and level in Africa is alarming and huge. This is because women abuse and suppression rate in Africa is much higher than any other continent. And the land (earth of Africa) would also rise to defend, support, or avenge the women of all evil done against them.

This is the reason why Africa land will not yield her full strength to our Africa leaders. Foreigners come to Africa to rule and do business, They are highly successful and prosperous. And Africans who go to other continents prosper.

<u>Jeremiah 22:29 – 30</u>

O earth, earth, earth, hear the word of the LORD. Thus saith the LORD, Write ye this man childless, a man that shall not prosper in his days: for no man of his seed shall prosper, sitting upon the throne of David, and ruling any more in Judah.

At a certain time, giving birth to female children was unwelcoming in our society. Those times, families prayed to have male child as their firstborn. Women who gave birth to female children only were tagged as enemies of progress and some ended up being thrown out of their husbands' house because they gave birth to female children.

Check the churches also. In the early days when women were strictly restricted from certain roles in the church, the church was as poor as rats and poverty was the church's second name. It would interest you to know that riches and wealth started manifesting in the church during the times and generation that permitted women some level of freedom to participate in church leadership roles.

Our lord Jesus enjoyed the ministry of women. Namely, Mary, Martha and the woman by the well who constantly make provisions to supply Jesus' needs. The woman with the alabaster oil was so much opposed by people around not because she did anything wrong but mainly for her gender. If the same oil had been poured on Jesus by a male, the same people would have praised him and spread the fame abroad.

Jesus saw through them, he knew they used the poor as an excuse but responded to them according to their folly. For the poor you will always have around you and that anywhere the gospel is preached what the woman did and her contribution to the propagation of the gospel would be mentioned.

Matthew 26: 7 - 13

There came unto him a woman having an alabaster box of very precious ointment, and poured it on his head, as he sat at meat. But when his disciples saw it, they had indignation, saying, To what purpose is this waste? For this ointment might have been sold for much, and given to the poor. When Jesus understood it, he said unto them, Why trouble ye the woman? for she hath wrought a good work upon me. For ye have the poor always with you; but me ye have not always. For in that she hath poured this ointment on my body, she did it for my burial. Verily I say unto you, Wheresoever this gospel shall be preached in the whole world, there shall also this, that this woman hath done, be told for a memorial of her.

By pouring the alabaster oil on Jesus, she prepared his body for his burial. Without what she did, the gospel and mission of Jesus was not complete. Because the death, burial and resurrection of Jesus is the complete gospel. His burial and resurrection confirmed his death.

Jesus was making the people know that women have a very crucial place and role in the gospel of the Kingdom of God. and they should not be despised or tamed or restricted.

In the last days, women will be involved in preparing the church in unique ways for revival and the second coming of Jesus. Just as she prepared the body of Jesus for burial, she will also prepare the body of Christ for rapture. No woman should be denied their inheritance or rights in the body of Christ.

Like what happened in the time of Moses. The tribe of Manasseh was going to be denied their inheritance because Manasseh had no sons, only daughters but God Almighty stepped in and instructed that the daughters of Manasseh were entitled to their inheritances and should be accorded the same privileges as with sons in other tribes.

Numbers 27: 5 - 7

And Moses brought their cause before the LORD. And the LORD spake unto Moses, saying, The daughters of Zelophehad speak right: thou shalt surely give them a possession of an inheritance among their father's brethren; and thou shalt cause the inheritance of their father to pass unto them.

The kingdom and the things of God are not gender based. For instance, can we say that because the tribe of Manasseh lacks male children, no church should be built in their land or that no apostle of the gospel should be raised among them. Since women were not allowed to have rule over a man in the church and not allowed to talk in the church. So please know that God is sovereign.

We are a chosen generation, a holy nation, a royal priesthood called to offer spiritual sacrifices acceptable unto God. The quick question is:

Does this scripture refer to men as the only chosen generation, or a holy nation, a royal priesthood called to offer spiritual sacrifices acceptable unto God ? Nay. It means also that our women are also a chosen generation, a holy nation, a royal priesthood called to offer spiritual sacrifices acceptable unto God.

It is the same Holy Spirit in the man that is also in the woman. We are both the temple of God. The Holy Spirit won't say because this is a woman, I won't use her or manifest through her maximally if she yields.

Chapter 3

Wealth, honor, and glory transfer

The actions and effects from biblical history could help us to understand the impacts of an undisciplined lifestyle towards another man's wife or properties. We would be reading a lot of scriptures here in this chapter.

Proverb 6:25

Lust not after her beauty in thine heart; neither let her take thee with her eyelids.

The kings considered in our case studies coveted and took a married man's wife and were captivated by a woman's beauty.

Matthew 5:28

But I say unto you, That whosoever looketh on a woman to lust after her hath committed adultery with her already in his heart.

- They coveted and took a married man's wife.
- Were captivated by a woman's beauty.
- They did not denounce the queenship rights and its privileges after returning the man's wife.

They did not denounce the queenship rights and its privileges after returning the men's wives to their husbands.

Adultery can be committed physically or lustfully. Jesus said if you look at a woman lustfully, you have committed the sin of adultery. As a matter of fact, any foolish thoughts or imaginations is a sin Prov 24: 9.

<u>Proverb 5: 9 – 10, 15 – 19</u>

Lest thou give thine honour unto others, and thy years unto the cruel: Lest strangers be filled with thy wealth; and thy labours be in the house of a stranger; Drink waters out of thine own cistern, and running waters out of thine own well. Let thy fountains be dispersed abroad, and rivers of water in the streets. *Let them be only thine own, and not strangers' with thee. Let thy fountain be blessed: and rejoice with the wife of thy youth. Let her be as the loving hind and pleasant roe; let her breasts satisfy thee at all times; and be thou ravished always with her love.*

<u>Proverb 6: 27 – 29</u>

Can a man take fire in his bosom, and his clothes not be burned? Can one go upon hot coals, and his feet not be burned? So he that goeth into his neighbour's wife; whosoever toucheth her shall not be innocent.

He that sleeps with his neighbor's wife has put fire in his bosom, and walked barefooted on hot coals, his clothes and feet are surely burnt, and he is no longer the same or complete. For he shall **<u>lose all the substance</u>** of his house including the throne and his glory.

<u>Proverbs 6: 30 - 33</u>

Men do not despise a thief, if he steal to satisfy his soul when he is hungry; But if he be found, he shall restore sevenfold; he shall give all the substance of his house. But whoso committeth adultery with a woman lacketh understanding: he that doeth it destroyeth his own soul. A wound and dishonour shall he get; and his reproach shall not be wiped away.

- Their wealth and generational wealth transferred to the victim's generation.

- Their generation shall always be smaller and of less greatness to that of their victims. Their generation shall bow before the generation of the afflicted.

- The land of philistines became that of Israel or Sarah's children by right for afflicting Abraham. So, by right, Joseph and Moses ruled in Egypt.

Isaiah 60: 14

The sons also of them that afflicted thee shall come bending unto thee, and all the that despised thee shall bow themselves down at the soles of thy feet, and they shall call thee, The city of the Lord, the zion of the Holy One of Israel.

King David as a case study

Let us examine how David was impacted with this issue as related to coveting another man's wife.

2 Samuel 11: 1 – 5, 14 – 15, 24

And it came to pass, after the year was expired, at the time when kings go forth to battle, that David sent Joab, and his servants with him, and all Israel; and they destroyed the children of Ammon, and besieged Rabbah. But David tarried still at Jerusalem. And it came to pass in an eveningtide, that David arose from off his bed, and walked upon the roof of the king's house: and from the roof he saw a woman washing herself; and the woman was very beautiful to look upon. And David sent and enquired after the woman. And one said, Is not this Bathsheba, the daughter of Eliam, the wife of Uriah the Hittite? And David sent messengers, and took her; and she came in unto him, and he lay with her; for she was purified from her uncleanness: and she returned unto her house. And the woman conceived, and sent and told David, and said, I am with child.... And it came to pass in the morning, that David wrote a letter to Joab, and sent it by the hand of Uriah. And he wrote in the letter, saying, Set ye Uriah in the forefront of the hottest battle, and retire ye from him, that he may be smitten, and die.... And the shooters shot from off the wall upon thy servants; and some of the king's servants be dead, and thy servant Uriah the Hittite is dead also.

David slept with Urias wife. Killed Uriah and married his wife Bathsheba.

<u>2 Samuel 12: 10, 24</u>

Now therefore the sword shall never depart from thine house; because thou hast despised me, and hast taken the wife of Uriah the Hittite to be thy wife. And David comforted Bathsheba his wife, and went in unto her, and lay with her: and she bare a son, and he called his name Solomon: and the LORD loved him.

- David slept with Urias wife.
- Killed Uriah and married his wife Bathsheba.

David disobeyed five (5) out of 10 God's commandments in a row.

- Thou shall not kill.
- Thou shall not commit adultery.

- Thou shall not covet thy neighbor's wife or properties.

- Thou shall not steal (David stole Urias wife)

- Thou shall not bear false witness against thy neighbor. (The letter of David to Joab in the war front was a false witness against Urias, he gave impression that Urias did something wrong that warrant death)

Let assume David never committed these evils, you would agree with me that one of David's sons from his wives would have been made the king after David reign.

You see, anytime you covet or sleep with another man's wife, the wealth, the labors, the honor, the glory, the position, and strength of your household is transferred to the stranger or inherited by the descendants of the woman you committed adultery with.

Your descendants would end up serving the descendants of the woman (a total stranger). With what David did, it is automatic, his wealth and glory has been transferred and concluded in the realm of the spirit. If David had not married Uriah' wife, the throne would have been taken away from David' and the descendants of Bathsheba would still have ruled Israel just because of the adultery. So, when God said do not covet your neighbor's wife, it was a serious issue.

David's wealth and kingship would have become that of Uriah's generation had David not killed Uriah and married his wife.

Little wonder why God made Bathsheba son, Solomon inherits the throne and wealth of David for a sin of adultery, for sleeping with a married woman.

1 King 1: 28 - 35

*Then king David answered and said, Call me Bathsheba. And she came into the king's presence, and stood before the king. And the king sware, and said, As the L*ORD *liveth, that hath redeemed my soul out of all distress, Even as I sware unto thee by the L*ORD *God of Israel, saying, Assuredly Solomon thy son shall reign after me, and he shall sit upon my throne in my stead; even so will I certainly do this day. Then Bathsheba bowed with her face to the earth, and did reverence to the king, and said, Let my lord king David live forever. And king David said, Call me Zadok the priest, Nathan the prophet, and Benaiah the son of Jehoiada. And they came before the king. The king also said unto them, Take with you the servants of your lord, and cause Solomon my son to ride upon mine own mule, and bring him down to Gihon: And let Zadok the priest and Nathan the prophet anoint him there king over Israel: and blow ye with the trumpet, and say, God save king Solomon. Then ye shall come up after him, that he may come and sit upon my throne; for he shall be king in my stead: and I have appointed him to be ruler over Israel and over Judah.*

1 Chronicles 22: 6 – 17

*Then he called for Solomon, his son, and charged him to build a house for the L*ORD *God of Israel. And David said to Solomon, My son, as for me, it was in my mind to build an house unto the name of the L*ORD *my God: But the word of the L*ORD *came to me, saying, Thou hast shed blood abundantly, and hast made great wars: thou shalt not build an house unto my name, because thou hast shed much blood upon the earth in my sight. Behold, a son shall be born to thee, who shall be a man of rest; and I will give him rest from all his enemies roundabout: for his name shall be Solomon, and I will give peace and quietness unto Israel in his days. He shall build a house for my name; and he shall be my son, and I will be his father; and I will establish the throne of his kingdom over Israel for ever. Now, my son, the L*ORD *be with thee; and prosper thou, and build the house of the L*ORD *thy God, as he hath said of thee. Only the L*ORD *give thee wisdom and understanding, and give thee charge concerning Israel, that thou mayest keep the law of the L*ORD *thy God. Then shalt thou prosper, if thou takest heed to fulfill the statutes and judgments which the L*ORD *charged Moses with concerning Israel: be strong, and of good courage; dread not, nor* *be dismayed. Now, behold, in my trouble I have prepared for the house of the* LORD *an hundred thousand talents of gold, and a thousand thousand talents of silver; and of brass and iron without weight; for it is in abundance: timber also and stone have I prepared; and thou mayest add thereto. Moreover there are workmen with thee in abundance, hewers and workers of stone and timber, and all manner of cunning men for every manner of work. Of the gold, the silver, and the brass, and the iron, there is no number. Arise therefore, and be doing, and the* LORD *be with thee. David also commanded all the princes of Israel to help Solomon his son, saying...*

<u>1 Chronicles 29: 1</u>

Furthermore David the king said unto all the congregation, Solomon my son, whom alone God hath chosen, is yet young and tender, and the work is great: for the palace is not for man, but for the LORD *God.*

Solomon learnt from David's mistake. Solomon would rather marry 300 wives and have 1000 concubines than go after a married man's wife. Solomon's mistakes though were marrying foreign women who turned his heart away from God.

God causes evil men to gather wealth and to then transfer to a man that is good in His sight. Uriah was a very good man that feared the Lord.

<u>Job 31: 1 – 12</u>

I made a covenant with mine eyes; why then should I think upon a maid? For what portion of God is there from above? and what inheritance of the Almighty from on high? Is not destruction to the wicked? and a strange punishment to the workers of iniquity? Doth not he see my ways, and count all my steps? If I have walked with vanity, or if my foot hath hasted to deceit; Let me be weighed in an even balance that God may know mine integrity. If my step hath turned out of the way, and mine heart walked after mine eyes, and if any blot hath cleaved to mine hands; Then let me sow, and let another eat; yea, let my offspring be rooted out. If mine heart have been deceived by a woman, or if I have laid wait at my neighbour's door; Then let my wife grind unto another, and let others bow down upon her. For this is an heinous crime; yea, it is an iniquity to be punished by the judges. For it is a fire that consumeth to destruction, and would root out all mine increase.

<u>Eccl 2: 26</u>

For God giveth to a man that is good in his sight wisdom, and knowledge, and joy: but to the sinner he giveth travail, to gather and to heap up, that he may give to him that is good before God. This also is vanity and vexation of spirit.

Pharaoh, Sarah, and Abram

Here, Pharaoh and Abram experience is our focus and what happened thereafter.

<u>Gen 12: 15 – 16</u>

The princes also of Pharaoh saw her, and commended her before Pharaoh: and the woman was taken into Pharaoh's house. And he entreated Abram well for her sake: and he had sheep, and oxen, and he asses, and menservants, and maidservants, and she asses, and camels.

Gen 13:5

For all the land which thou seest, to thee will I give it, and to thy seed for ever.

Pharaoh married Sarah. At this point Sarai was automatically a queen of Egypt, while Abram was just nobody and a stranger.

Abram acquired wealth through Sarai greatness and blessings or opportunities as queen. As a matter of fact, the starting capital for Abram business and greatness was through Sarah's influence on wealth.

Yet in all these things Sarai called Abram Lord. Women should humble themselves even if they have or seem to have greater wealth than that of their husband. Pharaoh sent Abram out of Egypt after returning Sarah to Abram, without any evidence of revoking, or dethroning or denouncing the queenship that was bestowed on Sarah.

Sarah left Egypt still having her title as a queen intact.

<u>Gen 12: 18 - 20</u>

And Pharaoh called Abram and said, What is this that thou hast done unto me? why didst thou not tell me that she was thy wife? Why saidst thou, She is my sister? so I might have taken her to me to wife: now therefore behold thy wife, take her, and go thy way. And Pharaoh commanded his men concerning him: and they sent him away, and his wife, and all that he had.

Abimelech, Sarah, and Abram

<u>Gen 20: 1 – 2, 14 - 16</u>

And Abraham journeyed from thence toward the south country, and dwelled between Kadesh and Shur, and sojourned in Gerar. And Abraham said of Sarah his wife, She is my sister: and Abimelech, king of Gerar sent, and took Sarah.... And Abimelech took sheep, and oxen, and menservants, and women servants, and gave them unto Abraham, and restored him Sarah his wife. And Abimelech said, Behold, my land is before thee: dwell where it pleaseth thee. And unto Sarah he said, Behold, I have given thy brother a thousand pieces of silver: behold, he is to thee a covering of the eyes, unto all that are with thee, and with all other: thus she was reproved.

Again, Sarah was snatched from Abram and crowned a queen in another kingdom called Gerar. For every country Sarai appeared or stepped into she was crowned a queen. And by such rights, she established the rights of her future generations, children, grandchildren, and great-grandchildren to rule in these countries. \

<u>Gen 20: 15</u>

And Abimelech said, Behold, my land is before thee: dwell where it pleaseth thee.

The king gave Abram rights to the land. Abimelech again gave Abraham wealth for Sarah's, his queen, the queen of Gerar sakes. And gave money (1000 shekels) for Abraham to keep an eye and watch over Sarah.

<u>Gen 20: 16</u>

And unto Sarah he said, Behold, I have given thy brother a thousand pieces of silver: behold, he is to thee a covering of the eyes, unto all that are with thee, and with all other: thus she was reproved.

Note his words: I have given your brother …. Your husband ….

I believe that Sarah was the first woman to demonstrate or show what God meant by the word "Help Meet". For the greatness of a man lies on the complete support from the woman or on the fulfillment of the woman's role.

Chapter 4

Generational Impacts of Kings' Adulterous Acts

Here, I would like us to study the effects and impacts of these adulterous thoughts or actions of these kings (Pharaoh and Abimelech) on their future generation. I will be looking at Isaac and Rebecca, Joseph, and Moses.

Rebecca and Isaac Case study

<u>Gen 26: 1 – 3, 6 – 13</u>

And there was a famine in the land, beside the first famine that was in the days of Abraham. And Isaac went unto Abimelech king of the Philistines unto Gerar. And the LORD appeared unto him, and said, Go not down into Egypt; dwell in the land which I shall tell thee of: Sojourn in this land, and I will be with thee, and will bless thee; for unto thee, and unto thy seed, I will give all these countries, and I will perform the oath which I sware unto Abraham thy father; ...

And Isaac dwelt in Gerar: And the men of the place asked him of his wife; and he said, She is my sister: for he feared to say, She is my wife; lest, said he, the men of the place should kill me for Rebekah; because she was fair to look upon. And it came to pass, when he had been there a long time, that Abimelech, king of the Philistines, looked out at a window, and saw, and, behold, Isaac was sporting with Rebekah his wife. And Abimelech called Isaac, and said, Behold, of a surety she is thy wife; and how saidst thou, She is my sister? And Isaac said unto him, Because I said, Lest I die for her. And Abimelech said, What is this thou hast done unto us? one of the people might lightly have lien with thy wife, and thou shouldest have brought guiltiness upon us. And Abimelech charged all his people, saying, He that toucheth this man or his wife shall surely be put to death. Then Isaac sowed in that land, and received in the same year an hundredfold: and the LORD blessed him. And the man waxed great, and went forward, and grew until he became very great:

Isaac went through the land of Gerar on his way to Egypt, but God intervened.

King Abimelech this time was very careful and allowed enough time to study the strangers. Recall Abraham and Sarah had once lied to Abimelech. He then discovered they were not brother and sister but husband and wife.

Gen 26:8

And it came to pass, when he had been there a long time, that Abimelech, king of the Philistines, looked out at a window, and saw, and, behold, Isaac was sporting with Rebekah his wife.

The king opened the whole land for them. Recall that Sarah was once a queen of Gerar. Who had a part in the land. So, Isaac sowed in the land as instructed by God.

Abimelech later entered a covenant of peace with Isaac and Philistines.

Gen 26: 26 – 29

Then Abimelech went to him from Gerar, and Ahuzzath, one of his friends, and

Phichol, the chief captain of his army. And Is, seeing ye hate me, and have sent me away from you? And they said, We saw certainly that the LORD was with thee: and we said, Let there be now an oath betwixt us, even betwixt us and thee, and let us make a covenant with thee; That thou wilt do us no hurt, as we have not touched thee, and as we have done unto thee nothing but good, and have sent thee away in peace: thou art now the blessed of the LORD, Isaac said unto them, Wherefore come ye to me

Note that God promised Isaac the land of the Philistines (not only Canaan) in Genesis 26, because Sarah acquired it by queenship and by rights. So, it was never a coincidence that the descendants of Abraham ruled these territories.

Joseph a beneficiary

Joseph, being a descendant of Sarah, became a beneficiary of Sarah's queenship rights in Egypt, and so, had every right to rule Egypt. Moses as well enjoyed that privilege.

So, we should be careful of what we do, for there are consequences awaiting in the future. Which our descendants can either benefit or suffer from.

These are satanic effects of coveting another man's wife or properties. It is amazing how descendants of Abraham and Sarah kept ruling as governors and princes in strange lands even in slavery.

<u>Genesis 41:41 - 42</u>

And Pharaoh said unto Joseph, See, I have set thee over all the land of Egypt. Then Pharaoh removed the signet ring from his finger, put it on Joseph's finger, clothed him in garments of fine linen, and placed a gold chain around his neck.

After the reign of Joseph, God had to find a way to ensure that Abraham never lacked a man in the corridor of power in Egypt. So, He raised Moses for that purpose.Then God justified him and set him in power.

Brethren, be careful of what you do, what you allow because these things can eventually be the justification for your lifting or demotion.

Can you now see the repercussions of the mistakes of the Pharaoh and Abimelech in the days of Abraham and Isaac generations.

Thank you for taking the time to read this far. Let us give full support to our women in the church to operate freely in whichever position or office God has positioned them.

God bless you.

Milton Keynes UK
Ingram Content Group UK Ltd.
UKHW021123111124
451035UK00016B/1184